ICELAND:
THE GOLDEN CIRCLE

ICELAND: The Golden Circle

BLUE LAGOON, THINGVELLIR, LAUGARVATN,
GULLFOSS WATERFALL AND GEYSIR

By Marques Vickers

**MARQUIS PUBLISHING
TACOMA, WASHINGTON**

Copyright @2022-2023 Marques Vickers

All rights reserved. Copyright under Berne Copyright Convention, Universal Copyright Convention, and Pan-American Copyright Convention. No part of this book may be reproduced, stored in a retrieval system, or transmitted in any form, or by any means, electronic, mechanical, photocopying, recording, or otherwise, without prior permission of the author or publisher.

Version 1.2

Published by Marquis Publishing
InsiderSeriesBooks.com
Tacoma, Washington

Vickers, Marques, 1957

ICELAND: The Golden Circle
BLUE LAGOON, THINGVELLIR, LAUGARVATN, GULLFOSS WATERFALL AND GEYSIR

Dedication: To my daughters Charline and Caroline. Many thanks to my friends Sveinn and Marie Helene for hosting me and assisting in driving me to photo shootings.

TABLE OF CONTENTS

Iceland's Golden Circle

The Blue Lagoon
Thingvellir
Laugarvatn Cave
Gullfoss Waterfall
The Great Geysir and Strokkur

SOURCES AND ARCHIVES SOURCED

Icelandmag.com
GuideToIceland.is
Traverse-Blog.com
Icelandtrippers.com
Wikipedia.org
Outdoorproject.com

Iceland's Golden Circle

Iceland's Golden Circle is marketed as three stunning locations within the southwestern sector of the country. The three include the Thingvellir National Park, Geysir Geothermal Region and Gullfoss Waterfall.

The capital city of Reykjavik forms the far western extremity of the circle's arc and becomes an excellent launching point. Two additional attractions, the Blue Lagoon and Laugarvatn Cave have been added to this guide. Each has become popular visitation stops.

The Blue Lagoon has evolved into a paramount visit for tourists owning to its close proximity to Reykjavik (29 miles) and Keflavik International Airport (13 miles). Since opening as an international spa resort in 1999, the thermal ice blue waters have attracted indulgent soakers multi-nationally.

The closest attraction to Reykjavik is Thingvellir (25 miles), the ancient gathering site of the Icelandic parliament and judicial process. Continuing east approximately ten miles is the Laugarvatn cave, formerly inhabited by two families during the beginning of the twentieth century.

At the farthest eastern extremity only 72 miles away from Reykjavik is the Gullfoss Waterfall. Europe's largest cascades surge from the waters of the Hvita River into a gorge shaping the Gullfossgjufur canyon below.

Looping back nearly midway towards Reykjavik, the Geysir Geothermal area in the Haukadalur Valley provides hot springs and consistent geyser eruptions. The famed Strokkur Geyser has earned a reputation for reliable launches of boiling water and steam.

The Golden Circle may be easily navigated by car within a single day. Haste however is wasted. Each attraction merits thoughtful attention and appreciation. Traffic is fluid and the roads are well maintained. The majority of attractions are easily accessible even during inclement months.

The Blue Lagoon

The Blue Lagoon has evolved into arguably one of the world's premier spa locations. Within tourist circles and promotional vehicles such as *National Geographic*, it has become labeled a *Wonder of the World*.

Few will dispute the distinctiveness and aesthetics of the water body and surrounding lava fields. The attraction's origins have often become obscured to promote the marketing assumption that the facility is a *natural* phenomenon.

In fact, only the water is natural.

In 1971, the Svartsengi geothermal plant began construction. The location was situated in close proximity to the capital of Reykjavik and Keflavik International Airport. It was completed five years later diversely employed for a variety of uses including heating and subterranean cooking.

For heating purposes, the boiling water is extracted directly from the ground and pumped into the radiators of residential and commercial buildings. The extracted water is approximately 392 F and loaded with dissolved minerals and seawater. The combination is unsuitable for direct piping due to corrosion. Instead, the water heats freshwater that is distributed into the urban network.

The original extracted water is afterwards released into nearby lava fields. The specific field surrounding the Svartsengi geothermal plant is called *Illahraun*, translated as Evil Lava. The lava's source is a volcanic eruption dated from 1226.

Lava is an exceedingly porous stone and the released water sinks into the crevices and cracks. The silica component within the water separates as it cools forming a muddy layer coating. Discharged water can no longer seep through the lava and ultimately rises into collective pools and passageways.

Thus began the genesis of the famed Blue Lagoon.

The original bathers began sneaking onto the property shortly following its completion. A young man with a severe case of psoriasis in 1981 became the first documented patient to soak in the waters to relieve his skin condition. The algae content reportedly enhanced his recovery. That individual, Valur Margeirsson christened the complex *Blaa Lonid* (Blue Lagoon) and the designation remained.

The first public bathing facilities were opened in 1987 and promoted towards patients with skin problem. By 1999, the growing popularity necessitated the development of expanded spa operations. The entirety of the present lagoon is an estimated 94,000 square feet filled with 9 million liters of geothermal seawater. The temperature remains a steady 102 F, but stretches of the water may fluctuate slightly in temperature.

The contemporary resort accommodates approximately 4,000 visitors daily. Admission prices have steady escalated to a base entry fee of nearly $100 USD. Lower promotion pricing exists, but predicated on season and admission entry times.

There is absolutely no apparent slackening of demand. Reservations are mandatory and pre-paid. Mid afternoon arrival time slots tend to sell out first. Visitors are allowed a stated one-hour arrival window based on their designated reservation time. Delays beyond the hour may result in the forfeiture of admission fees.

An estimated 1.5 million guests attend annually. It will surprise no one if that capacity continues to expand.

To understand the immensity of the Blue Lagoon operation, consider it simply the planet's largest soaking spa.

The party atmosphere is punctuated by recreational drinking (with imposed limitations), rampant selfie and group photography, complimentary silica clay masks and substantial noise. Thankfully for those pursuing a more sedate and meditative environment, a designated *cellular free* section exists, distant from the maddening crowd.

Aside from the waters, there exists a skin care and health product shop, restaurant and bar. Many locals have bemoaned the reality that *their* Blue Lagoon is no longer freely accessible to them. They are correct. Based on the demographics, the facility has become a lucrative enterprise targeting foreigners with zero expectation that will ever likely alter course.

Thingvellir

Thingvellir was the gathering site of the *Althing*, an annual parliament of ancient Iceland. The festivities were staged beginning in 930 AD until the final session in 1798. The Law Council established a structure of order and legal precedent.

The gathering of tribes and chieftains were weighty matters, far more than merely executive bureaucracies. From its infancy until the 15th century, the Council gathered on the east bank of the Oxara River. By 1500, the river had shifted course. The guardians simply relocated to an inlet within the river contour. In 1594, the Law Council was once again changed to the foot of the ancient Law Rock where it would remain for the next two centuries.

Power was distributed primarily amidst the tribal chieftains. Such an arrangement remained suitable until fissures emerged inciting family conflicts. Accompanying strife resulted in Iceland being governed under the Norwegian crown. Control ultimately shifted beyond the parameters of the island kingdom. The result was the King of Denmark being elevated into the absolute monarch of Iceland in 1662.

Thingvellir became the spiritual and cultural adhesion for Iceland. The annual two-week assemblage attracted thousands from a sparsely populated and disbursed kingdom. Temporary dwellings composed with walls of turf and rock were constructed with interim roofs of homespun cloth. The gatherings became a magnet for merchants, performers, craftsmen, farmers, beggars and dreamers. The festival became a unifying foundation for language and literature and emerged as a nationalistic icon.

The highlands are chiseled crags of volcanic stone seemingly suspended above lush and intoxicating plains below. The parkland plains designate the crest of the Mid-Atlantic Ridge forming the geographical boundary between the North American and Eurasian tectonic plates. To the south lies Thingvallavatn, the largest natural lake within Iceland.

As contemporary dusk settles like a curtain on the elevated stones and lava beds, it requires only scant imagination to reconstruct the past. The mist of history may shroud memory, but the sheer natural splendor still evokes imagination. The chieftain ghosts and their phantom legions still patrol amidst the crevices, proud, stiff and eternal. The echo from the winds reconstructs their presence, which is a sound that one feels rather than hears.

The guardians have never neither left nor receded in compromise. They govern the shadows atop their flinty cathedrals of grandeur. Their lasting authority remains unquestioned and unchallenged.

Laugarvatn Cave

Man-made caves have been employed as refuge for outlaws for centuries. The Cave of Laugarvatn became an exception to this role as it was designed from the outset for habitation. In 1910, a young couple, Indridi Gudmundsson and Gudrun Kolbeinsdottir, decided to inhabit the cave for eleven months. preferring the isolation and tranquility to traditional turf houses.

Indridi was a carpenter by trade and initiated the excavation of manure and rocks from two preexisting caverns. A kitchen and living room were installed in the larger space and sheep were housed in the smaller cave. The couple raised cows and horses on the property and sold their garden produce in Reykjavik

During the summer months, they erected a sizable tent and sold coffee, bread and cakes to travelers. Another couple, Jon Torvardsson and Vigdis Helgadottir later moved into the caves and resided there between 1918-1922. Jon was likewise a carpenter and sealed off the entrance. He installed a room with fresh paneling enhanced by a stove.

Their four-year stay resulted in the birth of three children. Two were born within the confines of the cave. In one instance the choice of birth location was necessitated by a raging blizzard outside.

During the subsequent decades, tales of haunting and the presence of protective elves have dominated the cave legacy. Danish King Christian X traveled to Iceland in 1921 and paid a courtesy visit. He was treated to a local delicacy of *Skyr Med Rjoma* (Icelandic Skyr with cream).

Visitors to the cave today are welcomed by a seasonally opened coffee shop. Visitors with a proper attitude, respect and homage towards local heritage may encourage the company of mischievous elves. The elves are reputed to be playful and not limited to physical apparitions. Many reportedly have invaded visitors' dreams during the slumbering hours.

Gullfoss Waterfall

Gullfoss Waterfall is Europe's largest and Iceland's most spectacular cascade. *Gullfoss* translates into Golden Falls.

The surging waters of the Hvita River stream from the glacier Langjokull before sheering off abruptly 36 feet down Gullfossgjufur Canyon. A second descent continues with a spectacular 69-foot plummet into the gorge below. The unusual duo split offers a rare perspective of seemingly two separate waterfalls.

The two cascades disappear underground into the basalt canyon as foaming froth. The canyon was originally fashioned by glaciers. The view is exclusively top down. Stationing any spectator viewing perspective from directly below the falls becomes both dangerous and nearly impossible.

The picturesque strata and multi-level cascades have attracted tourism since the mid-nineteenth century. A local farmer named Tomas Tomasdottir owned the land. An ambitious English businessman identified only as Howell attempted to purchase the property in 1907. His designs included establishing a hydroelectric plant and potentially other regional commercial development.

Tomasdottir refused to sell, but consented to lease the property unaware of a legal loophole. Howell intended to exploit this ambiguity to further his intended ambition. He may have outwitted Tomasdottir, but not his daughter Sigriour who would thwart his proposal. With unflinching resolve and energy, she hired a lawyer with her own limited funds to legally nullify the lease agreement.

The case staggered on for years necessitating her to travel periodically on foot to Reykjavik for legal proceedings. She ultimately prevailed and Howell abandoned his project. In 1979, Gullfoss was designated as a nature reserve enabling permanent preservation solely as a public viewing attraction.

The Great Geysir and Strokkur

The Haukadalur Valley is renowned for its abundance of hot springs and geysers. Lesser know is that the origin of the term *geyser* is Icelandic. The original verb *geysa* means to gush.

The two most celebrated geysers located within the thermal field are named the Great Geysir and Strokkur. Geysir rose to prominence during the nineteenth century. Reports indicated that by 1845, it was consistently erupting to a height of 560 feet. Towards the close of the twentieth century, it steadily became dormant.

An 1896 earthquake resulted in a reawakening multiple times daily, sometimes each exceeding an hour in length. By 1916, the eruptions had become nearly extinguished once again. In 1935, man-made efforts were initiated to stimulate activity. A channel was dug through the silica rim around the edge of the geyser. The ditch lowered the water table and stimulated a revival in activity. An even further desperate measure of adding soap was employed during the 1980s. A decade later, the practice was discontinued due to environmental concerns.

Periodic clearings of the channel have liberated Geysir, but as the passageway becomes clogged with silica, eruptions have become infrequent. Activity has been predominantly stilled since 2005.

Strokkur has evolved into region's most prolific and consistent attraction. Boiling water sourced from within the earth is hurled into the atmosphere between 65-130 feet high at intervals frequently interspaced only five to ten minutes apart.

Regional thermal activity has existed reportedly in excess of 10,000 years. The oldest human records date back to 1294 prompted by a series of regional earthquakes that altered the landscape. In 1630, a succession of violent geysers reportedly shook the accompanying topography with intense fury.

A local farmer owned the property until 1894. Periodic attempts to mine tourism gold and charge admission access were abandoned in 1935. The estate was sold to film director, Sigurour Jonasson. He generously donated the property to the Icelandic people in perpetuity enabling unlimited complimentary access.

INSIDER SERIES BOOKS.com

Author, photographer and visual artist Marques Vickers was born in 1957 in Vallejo, California. He graduated from Azusa Pacific University in Los Angeles and became the Public Relations and Executive Director for the Burbank, California Chamber of Commerce between 1979-84.

Professionally, he has operated travel, apparel, wine, rare book and publishing businesses. His paintings and sculptures have been exhibited in art galleries, private collections and museums in the United States and Europe. He has previously lived in the Burgundy and Languedoc regions of France and currently lives in the South Puget Sound region of Western Washington.

He has written and published over one hundred books spanning a diverse variety of subjects including true crime, international travel, social satire, wine production, architecture, history, fiction, auctions, fine art, poetry and photojournalism.

He has two daughters, Charline and Caroline who reside in Europe.

Printed in Great Britain
by Amazon